MW01284157

# KEEP IT ROLLIN

By: James "Jamey" Breen

# From The Editor's Desk:

I must say KEEP IT ROLLIN was a joy to read from start to finish. It is a window into the soul of a man who does not let adversity keep him from positivity. What is beautiful about this work is it is RAW and REAL. What is compelling about this book is that even if you have not been through the carbon copy scenarios that are presented there are elements of each chapter that everyone can identify with making it UNIVERSAL. The more I read and worked on this book the more I believed in the PURE POWER POTENTIAL of a message such as this. Each chapter is a different aspect of the same journey called life. A TRUE RESPECT for the creative process can be seen through the attention to detail, word choice, structure and creativity. Jamey had VISION that came ALIVE with the written word.

I wish Jamey every SUCCESS HARD WORK CAN BRING AS POSSITIVITY ROLLS ON.

ENJOY!


~Kristin G. Frappier~
Editor of Keep It Rollin

# Dedication:

For My Brother Dan
You are my rock and the source of my strength, without you none of
this would be possible.
Stay Weird Bro

# I

# Setting the Scene

"I was put on this earth for a reason. My purpose is bigger than the greatest of my challenges (Jon Gordon). Everyone has a purpose some people spend their entire life trying to figure it out. Maybe this will help you to get started on your journey here is something to keep in mind, "We were put on this earth for a reason to live out our purpose, to be our greatest self and to do it courageously" (Steve Maraboll). So many of us are still trying to figure out what is the best use of our time and sometimes we never find that answer. If a person is genuinely putting value into the world and others breathed easier because of their presence in the world, they have found their purpose. These people should consider themselves lucky because they have found something that some people may never find and that is truly special.

My name is James. Breen, I am 24 years old. I am a motivational speaker and blogger from Boston Massachusetts. At birth, I was diagnosed Cerebral Palsy. In 2014, I graduated from Stonehill College. I have always wanted to be an advocate for those with disabilities. I have taken many steps to become more involved in my community however; my strongest voice is heard through my blogging which began in September following graduation. Writing has become an outlet that allows me to be creative and also display my passion for serving others. In my blogs you will find that I cover a variety of topics ranging from embracing disability, overcoming challenges, motivation, following your passions, and maintaining a "Big Picture Perspective". My hope is that this helps people remain positive regardless of where they find themselves in life.

While I touch on these topics you will also find my personal story woven into the discussion. This is done to make it more "real" for my readers. Throughout this book I will be taking you back to specific moments in my life. I want you to feel as if you were walking right beside me as the event was happening.  When I started writing I hope to reach as many people as possible. This still remains the ultimate goal. However; I now know that if you are fortunate enough to impact one person you have been successful.

At the end of each piece of writing that I post for my readers I close with the Hashtag "Keep it Rollin". This is done as a gentle reminder for them to push beyond any obstacle and persevere with a positive attitude. I know it is not possible to be positive all the time. What is possible is the Pursuit of happiness. Thank you for taking this journey with me I hope that you will find my words, insight and perspective helpful as you embark on your own journey of self-discovery and personal happiness.

Thanks guys,

Enjoy

"Keep it Rollin"

Jamey

# II.

# How It Started

"Sometimes being a brother is even better than being a superhero" (Marc Brown). I have much to be thankful for especially for the bond I share with my brother. My mission has been to help uplift and motivate people as best I can. Everyone has gifts to share with the world this is my story and how I choose to tell it. I've always been a very motivated individual. My brother and my family have given me the boost I need to reach heights I never thought I could. This is a tribute to them and to everyone who has supported my mission to empower others and to follow a greater purpose in life. Our paths may change as life goes along, but the bond between us remains ever strong.

Without a doubt, I feel blessed to be where I am in life. We are in the changing seasons of 2015. I am at a good place with my writing and speaking, I feel motivated and ready to contribute to my community in any way that I can. I have started down this path because I have fallen perfectly in between something that I love and something that brings me happiness and fulfillment. I cherish the feeling that comes over me when I see somebody in the audience "light up" after something I say resonates with them. Another special moment is when someone comes over to me at the conclusion of a presentation and they express that they connected with my message in a big way. A reassuring moment comes when I receive those emails, comments and testimonials telling me to keep going. When people show their appreciation and gratitude, it lets me know that I must be doing something right. I am confident that I will continue going down this path and I will make what I am doing into my career. I will not let this opportunity to make a positive difference in the world pass by.

How did I get here? Where did all this positivity and motivation come from? To truly understand we have to back to 2013. In October of that year my world was turned upside down. My older brother Dan passed away in a car accident. I knew I wanted to carry on his legacy in any way that I could. This is why I started blogging and speaking. At this point, I will not go into very much detail of our relationship. You will learn much more of the bond between Dan and I throughout the rest of the book. Dan's death truly made me realize I wanted to motivate others. I wanted to show people how to be positive. I wanted it to be contagious. Simply put the real lesson here is to take a "step back" have an appreciation for your life because it is a "gift". We all don't know how long it will last. Live every moment with a purpose. Strive to have no regrets! To be honest, I thought to myself if it was me whose time came too soon would I be happy with my life? Would I be satisfied with what I accomplished? Would I be able to find peace? These are some questions that I had but eventually I stop asking them and started solely focusing on living my life to the fullest. Asking why is something that a lot of people do. I know however that my brother would want me to move forward and I see that as my only choice. I'm thankful for the way I am every day. Looking back on my life to this point the only emotion that I feel is gratitude. My family, friends and people who have cared for me, have put me in the position to have a positive impact on the lives of others. Not to say that there are not days or specific times in my life that were not difficult, yet I was fortunate enough to have everyone around me to help me stay positive. Whether it was just a bad day, one of my twenty- three surgeries or the highs and lows of living with a disability, growing up the way I did you learn a lot about yourself very quickly.

Sometimes it feels like life throws everything at you at once. Sometimes you wonder "why me"?

After you let yourself feel those emotions, you have the choice to pick yourself up and move forward in the most positive way that you know how. The alternative is to fold in the face of adversity. Over the course of these life experiences you begin to understand yourself. Life shows what you are capable of. How far you can go and when you can afford to push yourself or show restraint. It's called "Maintaining a balance". Understanding yourself is difficult for many people. Coping is also a big issue for some of us. In many ways, I am thankful for how I grew up and everything I have endured. This is because it has helped me find that balance. I am a big believer in fate. I know that God has a plan for me. Trusting in that plan and emulating the mindset of people around me, especially my parents and my brother, has me excited and prepared for the future. It is all about looking at the "Big Picture "in life, this is what really matters.

# III

# Independence

I have a vision for where I want to be in the next to five to ten years, I am no different. I have goals and dreams just like everybody else. In my opinion, society is "A little behind the "8" ball" In terms of where their expectations are for people with disabilities. In fact, let's not limit ourselves to just talking about disabilities but let's open up the conversation to everyone. At some point in a person's life there comes a time where they just want to be independent and everything up until that point in their life has prepared them for that moment. The beautiful thing about the topic of independence is that it relates to everyone.

Yes, I am completely aware that I have Cerebral Palsy which in and of itself presents its own unique challenges. It may sound comical that I'm mentioning that I am aware of my disability. Trust me it's not! Many people with a diagnosed disability are still finding things out about themselves and understanding their capabilities. Many people are still struggling to find their identity. My disability does not define or change my life's destination. I still have the same plan and I still plan on achieving everything I set out to do and more. If you have the mindset to do it anything is possible. The truth is your results are influenced by the amount of effort you put in I know that I am no different than the next person therefore that is how I conduct myself, my family and friends know this as well that society puts limits on us as people with disabilities. I have just accepted the fact that I can operate independently from what society's confines, I know what I'm capable of and that's all that matters to me. Struggling with something and having challenges in our lives is something that is common between all people. I feel as though I have nothing to prove personally. I have accepted and embraced my disability and I am currently working to obtain a driver's license, entering the workforce and becoming successful in all my endeavors.

The fact that I have a disability does not affect my overall desire to be independent. It will not affect my ability to achieve my goal because when I set my mind to something I persist no matter what it takes. I think I speak for the majority if not all of the disabled population when I say do not underestimate us, do not put limits on us and do not lower your expectations for us. There needs to be a more inclusive society taking shape. People are often afraid of what is unfamiliar or new to them. The way that a more inclusive society becomes a reality is awareness. I believe we have made great strides but this is just the beginning. We (as a society) still have many goals to achieve. We cannot settle! Later on in this chapter I will take you through some of my major surgeries that I've had throughout the course of my life and take you along for the ride to experience my ongoing "independence" journey.

"Independence was always the number one goal. We knew as a family that we would do anything to help you get there. We wanted you to have many opportunities to be happy and successful as your brother. You are no different we wanted you to be confident in everything that you would do in life and not feel limited." - My Mom

I talked to my mom the other day about having a son with a so-called "disability". It's up to the mindset of my whole family and our efforts because I've always felt this way. From the very beginning, I felt supported, loved and I was always told I could do anything I put my mind to and I believe that wholeheartedly. This is the first and most crucial step to being successful! It doesn't matter what abilities you have or don't have if you believe, your mindset will be your fuel. Cerebral palsy is a chronic disability meaning it will not go away completely. I can always improve by being healthy with my diet and plenty exercise.

I have been lucky to have doctors who genuinely care about my well-being, I am 24 and throughout those years I've had twenty-three surgeries. Every one of them has in some way or another helped me to become more independent. I would be lying if I said I wasn't nervous about having these surgeries but I knew that in the long run my parents and everybody who cared for me had my best interest in mind and that eventually I would see the benefits. Looking back now I am eternally grateful for everything that I've been through because now I can say with 100% certainty that it's paying off. Between ten and twelve years of age I had full length casts on my legs. This is because I had extensive reconstructive leg surgery. These casts were orange and blue in color because I loved the Florida Gators basketball team. I am usually able to walk but I had to keep my feet up the whole time I was wearing the casts. I was in a reclined position constantly but not in a comfortable way. I had to rely completely on somebody else to move. Considering my independent mindset this was not enjoyable, it was hard to see the benefits. Years later was when I had the biggest and most life-changing surgery. In 2008, I underwent a surgery to enlarge my bladder allowing me to be more independent and go to college, without any issues. Looking back now I don't quite know why it took me so long to come to grips with having these life-changing operations. In the moment when you're faced with the choice it seemed intimidating. We had hoped that there would be a less invasive alternative to major bladder surgery but in the end I'm glad I decided to have the procedure. That surgery in itself opened up a lot of new opportunities. It lifted a huge personal weight off my shoulders and gave me a lot of confidence.

It just goes to show you sometimes you have to step outside your comfort zone and do things that make you uncomfortable in order to move yourself forward and to a better place. In the beginning of this chapter I opened with a quote from my mom, part of it read "we would do anything you get there". My parents and my brother stuck by their word. The whole time in grade school all the way up through high school my parents were my biggest advocates, they worked tirelessly to make sure I had all the tools necessary to succeed inside and outside of the classroom. The hope was that I would learn how to speak up for myself and carry the torch when I got older. The reality is that school systems aren't always fair for those with disabilities. I missed out on some education. Particularly in middle school due to accessibility issues. Gates Middle School was built in 1918 and had a poor excuse for elevator or any other lift to supplement giving me access to the bottom floor. It was a dark dreary elevator that shook every time it moved. It reminded me of the "Tower of terror" in Disney except it was not fun at all. I missed class often because of it and more importantly I missed out on time with my peers. My parents constantly talked to the school about getting it fixed unfortunately that never happened during my time there. I talk a lot about family so it would only make sense to mention the way my older brother fits into this big puzzle. He is a huge piece of this puzzle, he is the person I grew up emulating. In the neighborhood growing up with the other kids, he knew it was going to be hard for me to keep up. Yet, he would still help me keep up. When it was football I was the quarterback and stood there and threw the ball until my arm fell off. When we played soccer or hockey I was the goalie. I would kneel in between two cones blocking the ball with my body. To the person that didn't understand it could look like I was target practice, but in my mind I was just having fun like every other kid. I played baseball standing in my walker and swinging the bat with one hand. I was the best one handed hitter to ever play the game! I would stand against the garage taking swings at fastballs from my dad. Trying to hit it over the fence, across the street! Basketball turned into a passion. First time I heard the net snap I was hooked. I still love the game to this day. Basketball is such an important aspect of my life that it deserves its own chapter that describes its impact. When I am on the court, my disability does not exist. The biggest confidence boost I ever got was the fact that my brother would not play unless we could figure out a way that I could participate. I used to think it was so cool that my brother would not allow himself to play unless I was there just like everyone else.

It was huge having my brother there growing up, the other kids in the neighborhood definitely followed his lead and did not see my disability. In high school, my brother drove a white 2000 Dodge

Dakota truck with enough room for my wheelchair in the back. Most of our friends had houses that were not accessible. That did not stop me it just meant we had to get creative. Dan would pick me up and carry me on his back so that I could be with our friends. Watching Dan pick me up was unreal. He was like "Superman". When I was with Dan and our friends my confidence was at its highest. It was almost like my disability did not exist because of everybody's ability to overlook it and just see me as a person. It would take too many words for me to explain how influential Dan was in helping me achieve this. He did it without any effort at all and all he wanted was to see me smile. It was infectious to others and they followed his lead. Dan truly loved having me out with him we were a "Force to be reckoned with" Dan and all my friends allowed me to do things that I could never have imagined.

I heard somewhere that psychologically feeling as though you belong to a group or community adds years to your life and for me everyone made sure that was possible. Independence is the ultimate goal. I have made great strides since my early years, still I know there's more work to be done. You can never keep me down. I am motivated and ready to achieve my goals and dreams. In the words of Ray Lewis a retired football player formerly of the Baltimore Ravens, "if you aren't pissed off for greatness that means you're okay with just being mediocre". I know there is more to life than just being average. I am mindful that I have been set up for a great life and I will not let this opportunity pass by. I have been given many gifts to share with the world and the confidence to do so. I have a belief in myself. I will be completely independent. Success starts with believing in yourself. You only get one shot at life. You have got to take that initiative; nobody will do it for you. I definitely believe that I will "KEEP IT ROLLIN" for years to come. No regrets! Always forward.

# IV.

# The Nation Transformation

I can only have a positive impact on the world by transforming the one thing I have complete control over and that is myself (Unknown Author). College is one of transformative experience in someone's life; At least it was for me. All four years of college are important. The first two years I spent at Dean College. Dean has its place in my history. I believe that every person deserves the right to have their own version of a transformative experience. It was during these first two years that I learned how to be a self-advocate. I am grateful for every experience that I've had.

I believe that this quote perfectly illustrates what I'm trying to say "you are only confined by the walls you build yourself"~ James Goll.

Dean was a solid foundation and acted as building blocks for what was to come next. I believe I came into my own after transferring to Stonehill in 2012. I believe that was the beginning of my transformation, making the decision to leave. It was at Stonehill; I discovered my passion and came into my own. This was done by forcing myself to become a presence on campus. I found my place with the basketball team and it was amazing.

For any college student regardless of ability, it can be difficult to manage the decision-making and responsibility of being away from home. By the time I transferred I felt ready to take on a bigger challenge. As a student on the new campus you want to dive into as many things as possible. It can be overwhelming. In these changing times, I focused most of my energy on helping the basketball team and serving on the disability committee. These were my two major commitments. I took up healthcare and communications because I knew I wanted to be an active voice within the disability community when I graduated. I figured helping out on campus was a good place to start. On the basketball team I learned what it was like to be part of a brotherhood. I am basketball player however, this is different. You are not only teammates but you are family. The coaching staff always had the mindset that Stonehill Basketball is a "FAMILY". That statement means something to all of us, I personally cherish being part of something greater than myself. We care for each other on and off the court and I have gained the respect of that locker room. It was with the basketball team that I first discovered my abilities to be a motivational voice of positivity. It feels great to be able to lift up a group of guys who I will always consider brothers. We lean on each other for support and I am grateful to always have them. It was amazing to watch them on the court knowing that my words play a part in strengthening our bond.

During my second year on campus the presence of the basketball team in my life was even more monumental after the loss of my brother. It was an enormous lift for me emotionally to come back to campus knowing that they were there. I came back after three weeks towards the end of October right before the season started. I looked forward to the structure of practices and games because it kept my mind off reality. I immersed myself in basketball and school in an effort to maintain some happiness. It will always be special when Stonehill meets Saint Anselm on the court. Every time I walk into their gym or they come to ours Dan's presence surrounds me. I know he's with me every day but this is a whole other experience. I always get a little more "jacked up" for those games. . It feels good that the team recognized the personal importance of these games for me and I know they have my back.

My two years spent on campus at Stonehill were unreal. I grew in maturity, confidence and my vision became clear as far as what I want to do for the rest of my life. I studied healthcare and communications inside the classroom. Outside the classroom however, I also learned a tremendous amount about myself. I learned my value as a motivator and advocate on-campus. People in positions of influence took my recommendations very seriously and we were able to make some great improvements to campus life for those with limitations. Throughout my time in the "Nation" as we all called it; I tried to figure out how I would use my skills as a motivator, advocate and voice of positivity and mold it into a career. It would be hard to find that perfect job I thought but with the risk of getting too far ahead of myself I wanted to focus on graduating. That day came, May 18, 2014 I walked across the stage and received my diploma with everybody else. Given the events of the past year it was a great time of reflection. I wanted to appreciate how far I had come. I could now call myself a college graduate. I also had eyes for the future. Knowing that I made it through this past year I could do anything. Just because I graduated by no means am I satisfied! I will push to make myself better. I will share what resources and insight I have to elevate others just as Dan elevated me. I believe that a greater purpose is possible for anyone who wants it. That is why it is worth repeating a quote that is at the beginning of this chapter "You are only confined by the walls you build yourself". I will not only climb over these walls in my path but I will also bring others along on my ride to be an example of positivity and strength for those who need it. If you have a story why not share, allow yourself to be transformed. Stories can change lives!

# V.

# "Fire"

Basketball brings me unmatched happiness. When I am playing or coaching, the world stops, nothing else seems to matter besides the game. It also brings disappointment, more so when I am coaching rather than playing. When you're coaching there is only so much you can do to affect the outcome of the game. When you see your team lose, your heart just sinks inside your chest. This is part of the love affair I have with the game. You have to take the good with the bad, and try to do the best you can. You have to leave it all out there. As a coach there is nothing you appreciate more than when you know your team has given it all and even though you may lose a game, you take solace in the fact that you have no regrets. For example, Stonehill lost a tough first-round matchup in the 2014 Division II National Tournament. In retrospect we had a great year and there was a lot to be proud of. In the moments after you lose and the final buzzer sounds you would be hard-pressed to convince anybody in that locker room to be happy about anything. In a way that's a good thing because you know that you have a group of competitors that hate to lose. You know that you have a competitive person when they hate losing more than they love winning.

Despite all these feelings and emotions that basketball brings to the surface for me the number one reason why the game is a huge part of my life is because it gives me a competitive outlet to express my "Fire." What do I mean by that? "Fire" is an internal desire, an unrelenting competitive attitude. It is a cross between an endless enthusiasm and a deep rooted anger. Sounds bad right? It's not, it gives me a way to take everything that is bothering me in my life and put it towards something meaningful and positive. That is what makes a great competitor. A great competitor has the ability to take their focused aggression and throw themselves into the fire.

It ignites in "pre-game" when you run/roll out for warm-ups. You look down at your arms and your body has goosebumps all over it. You go through the layup line a few times and your adrenaline starts flowing and your first sweat of the day forms on your back. It's one of the greatest worst feelings ever. Nerves are good as long as you can figure out how to control them. Your heart starts beating faster to the point where you can feel it inside your chest. This is also a good feeling because it's letting you know that your body is ready for anything you can throw at it. Always remember that the fire starts somewhere deep inside you. It's all about "how bad you want it". You might have to outlast the other team but that's okay because you know that you're willing to go beyond to give more than the other team. A leader is the person who's "Fire" is visible and contagious, making the rest of the team want to do and achieve more. The leaders passion helps sow the seeds of brotherhood, which is essential to team bonding and success. In order to operate on this level all thirteen players have to flow as a cohesive unit, a well-oiled machine. Every time I look at someone on the team I am reminded of my brother's presence by their different attributes. I am able to use this feeling to add fuel to my fire.

The greatest thing about my competitive "Fire" in basketball is that it translates into life. I cherish that as one of life's great lessons that I've gained from playing sports. If I can take all the feelings and emotions that I have when playing basketball and apply them to real- life situations, I will be successful. Everyone has a flame that burns within them. It's up to the individual, how they are going to keep the flame burning for years to come. All people have something to offer this world. They just have to possess the desire to get out there.

Here is a quote from a book that had a positivity impact on me called "Every day I Fight" by the late ESPN anchor Stuart Scott, Cancer does two things to you, it can kill you. It can also give you the strength to keep on fighting. Every day after chemo I made a promise to myself I would be in the gym working out a half an hour after one of my treatments. I would be in there throwing kicks and punches until I collapsed on the floor but that felt good." If that doesn't scream competitive "fire" I don't know what does!

Sometimes people with disabilities can feel as though they are limited due to this "Dis" ability. However, throughout the course of my life I have realized that this is just a false belief holding me back from what I truly want to accomplish. Our disabilities can cause us to live life with a "chip" on our shoulder that doesn't need to be there. Everybody wants their motivation to come from a meaningful place rooted in good intentions. In actuality, all you have to do is learn to embrace yourself. If you use all your "fire" trying to prove something you will never find what makes you happy. During my first year of college I was pumped to be on my own away from home. I was going to do everything for myself and not ask for help because during that time I felt like asking for help with the sign of weakness. I was determined to use my "fire" to be independent. A perfect example of this was when I went down to the cafeteria for the first time to eat dinner. I wanted grilled chicken and salad, I was in my wheelchair and the food was up too high for me to reach. I pulled myself almost to a standing position and stretched as far as I could reach to make the salad. After trying to do this for what seemed like an hour I thought about leaving without eating. Was I really going to let my frustration, pride an overwhelming need to be independent get in the way of me nourishing my body? After literally sitting there for several minutes thinking about this I decided to swallow my pride and ask for help. This may not seem like a big deal the average person however, for me it was a big breakthrough that would set the tone for the rest of my college experience. I realize that asking for help is not a sign of weakness rather a sign of strength. This was an opportunity for me to be a strong self-advocate. In that instance, I knew I possessed the desire to help others as well.

What does this have to do with basketball? You learn a lot about yourself from playing sports; independence, confidence, success and failure just to name a few. All of these things are important in shaping who you are. From the very first time my dad lifted me up to "dunk" the ball on the hoop in our driveway I have tasted success because of basketball. Sports transcend life. I was able to find success, acceptance and equality on the basketball court. Now it brings me confidence in my life as a whole. What's the overall message of this particular story? Use your "fire" to create your motivation for things that bring you fulfillment. Try not to waste valuable time and energy "proving something" Ask for help when you need it. Work on embracing yourself and living the life that you were given because you're the only on

# VI.

# Post-Grad

"Each day when I wake up I am thankful for the nights that turn into mornings. The friends that turn into family the dreams that become a reality and the person we like turns into love."~ Unknown Author

For me, this is a quote about two things, first treating each day as if it were a new opportunity for positive change and personal growth. These two things are vital to a brighter outlook on life. Secondly, as you change and evolve into the person that you are becoming be mindful of those who have supported you. Overall, this quote is about positive change and learning to embrace it. This notion resonates with me because I maintain a "big picture" perspective. I was always brought up to see the positive side of life, and when I graduated I started a mission to share that with others.

The time spent after college can be some of the most aggravating and discouraging months of someone's life. These days it's very difficult to get a job. For me, given everything that had happened in 2014 many of my friends and family said that just getting to graduation and walking across the stage was an accomplishment in itself. Don't get me wrong, I am very proud of everything I did that year I just knew that there is still more out there for me. I had a goal to graduate college in four years and I did just that. I wanted to have employment by the beginning of October that fall. That month held significance for me because it would have been special to start working around my brother's one year anniversary. Unfortunately, that did not happen and I had to reevaluate and just keep moving forward. Finding a job is just like anything else in life, you can't allow yourself to get down you have to refocus your energy and channel that frustration into something positive. I had applied to countless human services jobs I wanted to work in the disability community as advocate. Many times that I would send in an application via email and a few weeks later I would wonder why I didn't get a response. After a few times of this happening it can be a letdown. That is why it is very important to have self -confidence. Know what you are worth it and know what you can bring to the table. Some days will test your patience \and some days will shake you but not break you!

If you spend your post grad days emailing and just waiting for people to get back to you it can be very long and drawn out process. You have to be proactive and follow up and make sure people know you're interested. I wanted to make sure that people knew how interested I am and how motivated I am to work. It is all about showing initiative. The question you have to ask yourself is how are you going to separate yourself from others? How are you going to stand out? I chose to separate myself by using my talents for writing and speaking to start a presentation business telling my story and helping others. I thought this would be a great way for me to expand my community and meet new people. It also helps that one of my passions and also bringing personal fulfillment. If you cannot change something use it to your advantage. Not only does this bring me a sense of wholeness but it is also a great way for me to show people my capabilities and how I can be an asset to any organization.

What I have learned while navigating the challenges of postgrad life is that you have to identify your strengths and combine them. If you identify these areas you will be successful in carving out a passion driven business. I've learned while navigating the challenges of postgrad life that you have to identify your strengths and combine them. If you identify these areas you will be successful in carving out a passion driven business. I have heard people say often times that "You create your own luck based on how hard you're willing to work" (Unknown Author). I have taken my strengths and turned it into a business, something positive to help others. One of my favorite motivational movies of all time is "Miracle" The story of the 1980 USA Olympic hockey squad that competed in Lake Placid. One of the lines from the movie is fitting in this situation. The quote reads "Great moments are born from great opportunity" -Miracle. This offers great perspective, if you want great moments to happen in your life you cannot be afraid to sweat to achieve those great opportunities. They don't happen on their own. I believe if you put value into the world it has a way of coming back to you. So to all those people frustrated by trying to achieve their goals, just keep working you will get what's coming to you! In my presentations I have used the line "Sitting on our parents couch might be comfortable, it might be easy but it won't get you anywhere."

For me, moving forward is the only way to go. Everyone deserves an opportunity to define themselves and if you keep working you will define yourself and your own greatness. There is this belief going around the disability community that you're disability prevents you from working. I believe that if I can show good performance just like anybody else shows good performance then I am just as entitled to a job as the next person. This belief that disability prevents a person from working is just a limiting factor that we all need to put in our rearview mirror; I know that anything is possible.

I feel very fortunate to be in this position and I would like nothing more than to talk individually about each friend and significant person in my life. I am deciding against it, each friend is just as important as the next one. To devote more attention to one relationship is just unfair in my eyes. I truly appreciate every individual who has helped me for different reasons. I believe if you put positivity and value into the world it comes back to you. It seems that the right person has a knack for coming into my life at just the right time. I am truly thankful for everyone.

In the previous chapter, I had mentioned utilizing my skills as a motivator and advocate within the disability community. I decided to work on establishing myself as a motivational speaker; I also discovered I had a passion for writing. These two things seem to complement each other perfectly. Every person has a story and a message but what separates people is their ability to articulate it with the intention of helping others. I am blessed with the ability to tell my story in a way that helps others. As I have mentioned before, it started as a way of carrying on my brother's legacy. Thanks to word-of-mouth and the use of Facebook and Twitter my message has spread throughout many channels and across social media outlets.

In the beginning, it was difficult for me to stand up in front of the audience and talk about my life especially the events of the past year. As I got the opportunity to deliver more and more presentations the experience and message I was delivering was invaluable. The response I received from everyone begun to fill a hole in my heart. I found comfort in the fact that I was able to deliver compassion and positivity just as my brother did for me.

As I sit here writing I must acknowledge I have had the great privilege of visiting close to twenty-five locations to deliver my presentation. I have researched utilizing all the information I can gather about motivation. I do not claim to be an expert in this field; I don't believe that anybody is ever truly an "expert "because you never stop learning. It is about helping each other and sharing resources and information to help the growth of your community. There are many people out there on social media writing articles claiming they have the "key" to happiness or the "formula" to make a fortune. Some of these people even "guarantee" success. One thing I have learned about "guarantees" is that there are none, especially in life. Many of these people are either conducting business to make money or trying to launch a career in this field. I do my best to be "real" with people. I talk to people in a way that makes them feel comfortable and in a way that reassures them on the days of doubt that they will be successful despite the challenges they face. I try to keep in mind that I appreciate when people are "real" with me so I give it back to the people. This approach helps the message to be more genuine and helps people be more receptive to what you are saying. It is the message that paramount to all else. Don't get me wrong it's nice to be paid for your services. I promise you the readers here and now that is not and will never be the number one priority for me. My goal overall is to use my presentations as vehicles to ignite conversation and then for the people who hear me speak to carry on that momentum and use it in their own lives.

Ralph Waldo Emerson once said, "success is knowing that somebody else breathes easier because you have lived" I want to thank every organization that has given me the opportunity to present to their groups. I want you all to know that you are not only helping the groups you serve every day, you are also helping me to spread my messages positivity and motivation to as many as possible. I am truly grateful for every opportunity and I want to thank you from the bottom of my heart for making this dream a reality. The fact that so many people have started to believe in my message is the greatest feeling that I could ever ask for. I will leave no stone unturned! I will follow every opportunity to the end of its rope and I will "keep it rollin"! My hope is that people will start to embrace a holistic approach to life and focus on the bigger picture. I hope that people who have the opportunity to hear me speak embrace the pursuit of happiness, along the way finding their own version of success. If I can make a difference for one person I have done my job. I believe that stories are transformative forces! I know that positivity can be contagious!

# VII

# Disability?

"What lies behind us and what lies in front of us are small matters, what really makes the difference is what lays within us. Often times, the things we cannot change about ourselves are the things that change us for the better."~ Ralph Waldo Emerson I believe it says a lot about a person's character when they can honestly admit that they are comfortable with themselves. I am going to take that one step further and say that I am not only comfortable with myself but, I am grateful for my disability. Without it I would not be myself. I have never known anything different and I love it.

Learn to fly! Smash boundaries! Do not listen to stereotypes! Do not place limits on your potential always want more and never settle for less than what you were are worth. Back in college I took a class titled Disability? This class shed some light on common misconceptions and stereotypes surrounding disability. I personally got to know the professor very well and we had many conversations after class. One of the most profound things he ever said to me was

"Don't let people rent space in your head" I gained a lot from taking that class, I benefited more from just having his understanding outside of the classroom. It was helpful knowing I had someone who understood me as a person.

Make your disability or your challenge work for you. What does that mean? Take what is perceived as a weakness and turn it into one of your greatest strengths! My Cerebral Palsy makes it more difficult for me to physically do things as quickly or efficiently as someone without a disability. I have limitations and I'm fine with that. In fact, I love the person that I am. Why? I do not know anything else. I have been this way since I was born. Before I get too far into my feelings on disability I want to mention that throughout writing this book I had pondered whether to write a chapter solely dedicated to disability. My thought process was do I really want to make disability the entire focus of a chapter? I had reservations about it at first because in my mind my disability is not the focus of my life it is just a part of who I am and I have learned to embrace it

Then a few chapters into my writing process I had a change of heart. If I brought my disability to the forefront and talked openly, it would serve as an example for others helping them to embrace who they are. For me, this fits my mission perfectly to serve as a role model for those who need a little extra push. Sometimes people may lack the confidence to speak up for themselves, I want to be the voice for the people who cannot do it on their own. My ultimate goal however, would be to get them to a point where with enough coaching and support they could do it independently.

For the past two years I have had the privilege of attending a leadership conference in Bridgewater Massachusetts hosted by Bridgewater State University and put on by Easter Seals of Massachusetts. During my four days at this conference one workshop in particular stayed with me because its message was so powerful. In order to gain understanding spread awareness and help others sometimes it's necessary to open yourself up to show others that it's okay. That is exactly what these two people who ran the workshop did, they talked openly about positive and negative words and thoughts associated with disabilities. It helped everyone to see these two women open themselves up it also helped us because they too have disabilities which made it all more "real" for us. Sometimes these things are difficult to talk about and more often than not we don't bring them up because we're scared to put ourselves out there. It is not easy to bring yourself to admit that sometimes we doubt our ability to be successful Sometimes we feel worthless and think about throwing in the towel and giving up. Then the other side of the coin was positive things associated with disabilities and we listed all the positive words and feelings associated with being disabled.

The outcome of the workshop was to associate a positive word or feeling with a pebble which was given to us and every time we held that pebble we would think of that positive word and remember our experience at the conference. This feeling would help reenergized and refocus highlighting the positives in life. To be perfectly honest with you I know that the focus of the workshop was disabilities. This message applies to everyone because all people have challenges. Little reminders to re-energize and stay positive help us all to keep things in perspective. This message will always stay with me.

I have always been a team player and love the bond that is created between people involved. To me the disability community is one big TEAM!!! We all have our own individual goals but collectively we want to work together to move society forward and spread awareness and understanding of our population. The Americans with disabilities act is twenty- five this year. It was passed in 1990 and since then we have made great progress. I personally feel very proud to be associated with this movement and upward positive trend for the disability community. I want to go back to what my professor in college used to say, "Don't let people rent space in your head." What I think my professor meant by those words was it may take a long time for society to catch-up but if you have confidence in yourself, you have a great gift to share with others. Society may have low expectations for people with disabilities but is long as you have a belief in yourself there's no reason for negativity to creep in to your mind. Confidence is a great thing to have and it can bring a lot of opportunities your way if you are willingness to work with it

I feel fortunate enough to have spent the past year pursuing my passion. As a motivational speaker, my messages are of positivity; embracing challenges and turning your obstacles into opportunities for success is what life is all about. This will help us reach our fullest potential and be the best we can be. My message is one of positivity, embracing your challenges whatever they may be and reaching your fullest potential. I talk about embracing challenges because if we are being honest with each other challenges are a part of life. I am not overcoming my Cerebral Palsy I am simply living within its means and making the best of a life in a wheelchair. Your life is what you make of it. Through my speeches I help others to use what I am saying to enrich their own life. I want the information, knowledge, insight and resources I give them to be useful after I leave. The focus is not on and what I've been through as a person. The spotlight is on the audience and helping to make them better as people.

I want to be the person that starts a conversation that maintains itself for days and weeks following my presentation.

"Inspiration" is a word I personally choose not to use to describe myself. I do not deserve any extra credit, I am not special and I only desire to show others how far a little positivity can take them. Nothing is more personally gratifying than to see people leave one of my presentations all "Fired up." Knowing that I ignited somebody's fire is all the fulfillment I need. If people are going home a little more motivated because of what I was able to do in the short amount of time we were together is just awesome to me. Knowing that a person can now go home and make positive changes in their life is an unreal feeling.

I have had people in my life that have done for me what I am now doing for others. I believe that everybody deserves to have that support and to be given that extra push to be successful. I am grateful that I have been given the ability to do that for countless others. You never stop learning, adapting and gaining new knowledge, although I offer my support to others by no means do I know everything and I do not pretend to have all the answers. All I can do is share with others what has worked for me and do the best I can to offer my assistance.

The world would be a much better place if we all just focused on being more genuine and if we make a point to overlook disability and allowed ourselves to see the person inside. To me disability is a man-made concept reinforced by mainstream society, stereotypes and misconceptions. The reality is it will take a long time for society to fully embrace differences. My disability has given me great things, the most important being my outlook .on life. It has humbled me and helped me to appreciate the "little things". I know I have limitations and that is why I cherish my abilities and choose to focus on things I can do rather than the things I cannot. If a person asked me to summarize my ultimate goal in one sentence it would likely read: I wish to help all people to see life as a gift because every day is a good day no matter who you are. That is why I "Keep It Rollin". There's always a greater purpose what is yours?

# VIII.


# Emerging Leaders

John Maxwell once said," great leaders do not set out to be leaders… They set out to make a difference. Leaders do not become great because of their own power..... Their ability to empower others is what truly makes the greatest difference".

I lead from the sidelines. I do not need all the attention for myself. I know what I am capable of as a person and my goal is to empower others and help them achieve their dreams and stay positive. It's not about what I have done or what I have accomplished I am perfectly willing to play a minor role in order to see others succeed. In the process of becoming a leader in my own community, I have discovered my own ability to empower others to do the same I will lead by positive example and give others the tools they need and to become great leaders in their own communities. It's about moving society forward being progressive smashing boundaries and getting rid of stereotypes along the way if I have to play a small role for this to happen I will do it as long as it moves society in the right direction. These lyrics from Christian hip-hop and R&B artist Lecrae clearly illustrate what it is I'm trying to say:
"It's evident you run the show, so let me back down

You take the leading role, and I'll play the background

I know I miss my cues, know I forget my lines

I'm sticking to your script, and I'm reading all your signs

I don't need my name in lights; I don't need a starring role

Why gain the whole wide world, if I'm just going lose my soul

And my ways ain't pure if I don't live according to Your Word

I can't endure this life without your wisdom being heard

So word, to every dancer for a pop star. 'Cause we all play the

background, but mine's a rockstar. Yeah, so if you need me I'll be

stage right praying the whole world will start embracing stage fright.

So let me fall back, stop giving my suggestions 'Cause when I

follow my obsessions, I end up confessing. That I'm not that

impressive, matter of fact. I'm who I are, a trail of stardust leading to

the superstar I could play the background."

When you decide to put yourself out there with a message, you have to decide why you are doing it. Who is benefiting from hearing you? What is the ultimate mission? I have decided that this is my goal to use the gifts I have been given to move others forward and see people achieve happiness. For me it is amazing to see others believe in themselves, and if I can be one of the people who gets them excited for life, I am perfectly humbled to play on the sidelines

I have talked many times throughout the writing of this book about family. I am truly grateful for those people who have made a difference in my life, those people who have empowered me to keep going. I know that this encouragement has come from their hearts; I have risen to new heights because of their support. I am reflective and proud of how far I've come, but by no means am I satisfied. . I know that there's much more out there in the world for me to accomplish. How do you move forward? The answer is by always staying hungry and humble and realizing that nothing is given to you. Everything is earned with hard work and determination.

I want nothing more than to show others what I have learned. Just as I have been supported I now want to pay it forward and support others. There are too many people out there on social media making false claims. These people claim to "have the keys to running a successful business" or "5 ways to be happier". Lastly, I see this one a lot "Want to make a fortune? Use these steps to make your business run on auto pilot". There isn't a day that goes by where I'm not searching Twitter or Facebook and I see blog post on either one of these sites telling me how to drive more traffic to your social media pages. How to get more "retweets" "followers" and "likes". More often than not you have people competing to start businesses so they want to be the ones with the strongest "sales pitch" but have no genuine interest in helping people. I don't have all the answers; I do that know my words come from a good place. Too many people are concerned with "getting ahead" There's not enough sharing of resources, knowledge and insight to make the different that is needed. Where are our leaders with a sense of community and sincere interest in elevating not themselves, but others? Is it because some people have too much pride and think what they do is too important?

I am aware of my own limitations; the truth is everybody has them. If I have knowledge, insight or information that would help another person I will share it. I am interested in investing in the people to grow society. There may be some physical limitations involved but I am fully aware of what I "can do" and that will be my focus it always has been. I can be a voice for those who don't have one. I will also supplement this by acting on my greater purpose. I have a tremendous ability to motivate, advocate and bring out the positives in life. That is my greater purpose. That is my "bigger picture" and this is my way of being a leader!

Every single person has the capability to do this. It is about discovering where your strengths and weaknesses lie. Show a willingness to go out there and take control of what is yours. You do not have to be successful All anybody can ever ask of you is to make an honest effort. You do not have to do anything extraordinary. Be genuine, honest and humble set an example for others to follow this is the true essence of a leader. I do not claim to have all the answers, because I do not. What I can share you is what has made a difference for me. I will not hold back information insight and knowledge. I hope this can bring people together allowing them to find common ground and creating more of a sense of community. The desired outcome is to form a more holistic society with genuine and true values. I realize I cannot change the world overnight but hopefully this starts the conversation. At the very least know that you don't have to be some extraordinary human being to make a difference or to be a leader... you just have to be willing to try that's all anyone could ever ask. Once again always remember that "Great leaders do not set out to be leaders... They set out to make a difference. Leaders do not become great because of their own power..... Their ability to empower others is what truly makes the greatest difference

.

.

# IX

# I'M THE GREATEST

Somewhere I heard once "there is a very thin line between confidence and arrogance, confidence smiles arrogance smirks. Be humble in your confidence and courageous in your character."~ Unknown Author I have always been very confident and outspoken about my ability to be successful, but I was always told to have a conscience this keeps me humble in grounded. I strive to do great things, yet focus on always doing the right thing.

Judging by the title chosen for this chapter you might be thinking it comes off as a little conceited. Another thought you might be having is that I am trying to quote the great boxing champion Muhamed Ali. Both those thoughts are wrong, what I'm doing is starting a conversation about positivity, which is someone's ability to be positive a natural ability, a learned behavior or combination of both.

I would argue that it is both a natural ability and a learned behavior resulting from the environment in which a person is raised. Back in college I took a class on sports psychology, one of the units covered was called "Self-talk and mental toughness." I personally gained a great deal this particular unit "Mental toughness" and "self-talk" are terms used by coaches but the definition of these words are not always clearly defined. They can mean something different to each person who uses them. How I have heard them used is in scenario at the end of games when energy and focus is fading and teams need to re- -energize for the "final push" especially when team is down in fighting their way back. Coaches will say something along the lines of "come on! This is the point in the game where the more mentally tough team separates themselves we practice every day for situations like this.... leave it all out there! No regrets

A few chapters into this book I wrote a chapter called "Fire" In several ways this chapter and "Fire" are related. When you wake up in the morning and you can just tell that it's not going to be one of the best days, Can you still be positive, and can you still self-motivate and be productive? Some people can do this however, others need a little encouragement. If you are one of those people who can just walk into the bathroom every morning look at yourself in the mirror and tell yourself "I am the greatest", if you have the ability to block out negativity and just focus on the next positive thing in your life that is a gift and an amazing skill to have. The reality is that if you have this gift you should cherish it because everyone battles with self-doubt and their ability to be successful. If you can be somewhat self-reliant and talk yourself into a better frame of mind it helps significantly change your outlook and put you on the right path.

You might find that I make a lot of analogies between sports, being a part of a team and family. When you can't find the strength to get up every day to tell yourself "I'm awesome.... today is going to be a great day," you need your family, we need our team to have our back. Over time we get used to our team and our family having our back, then gradually we build confidence and learn to self- motivate and energize ourselves because we know that if we ever need them they will be there. They are the people that make up our team and have given us the confidence to try and to fly. At some point this happens for everybody but we are much better off if we have that foundation from the beginning. It is always good to have that "Safety net" even if we never end up needing to use it

On a personal note, I have always been a positive person. Growing up I had a great foundation behind me making it possible for me to be confident and embrace every challenge that was in front of me. I'm going to be honest I talk to myself a lot; I'm also am a very competitive person. I have always had the ability to "Pump myself up". When practicing basketball, I always wanted to take one more shot. I never wanted those long summer nights of playing basketball in the driveway to end. Even when my parents encouraged me to come inside because it was getting dark and the mosquitoes were coming out; I didn't want to leave because I was always competing with myself. It takes me back to a scene in my favorite childhood movie "Space Jam" The scene begins with you hearing the sound of a bouncing ball and the "Snap of a chain net and a younger Michael Jordan appears his father hears him playing outside realizing its late he tries to bring him inside. At that moment, Michael's dad realizes his son's passion for the game of basketball. Michael says to his father" One day I'm going to play for the University of North Carolina". Michael dad chuckles and says "OK son shoot till you miss." That scene reminds me of my summer nights in the driveway.

When I'm jogging in my walker back-and-forth down the street I always want to do an extra lap. My goal has always been five laps but I push for six. At the gym whoever I'm with whether it's my dad or one of my friends I push myself to do an extra set of every exercise. I realize my physical capabilities are limited but we make it work and I push myself not because I have something to prove, or because I have a desire to stand out, only because I get satisfaction out of competing with myself and getting better just like any athlete would. Instead of dwelling on things I cannot do I am thankful for the abilities I do have.

For me the most intriguing battle is the one going on inside myself. Being involved in sports for a good portion of my life I've heard this quote said in a million different ways, but essentially it goes like this "you're greatest and toughest opponent is within you". For me it doesn't take much for my "Fire" to be ignited, Whether I'm at the gym, on the court or just in my driveway shooting hoops, I'm competing with myself and whatever is on my heart motivates me to do more. In life, I'm doing my best to find the next "stepping stone" in my career because I believe that we all have a greater purpose. I will do what it takes to find mine!

I would be lying to you if I said I never doubted myself. That is why I am so grateful for my team and my family for always being there when I need them. Getting back to the original question at the beginning of the chapter, Is positivity a natural ability or learned behavior? For me it is most definitely a combination of both. I have the ability to push myself and motivate from within however I never would have gotten to this point in my life if it wasn't for my team and my family. These two things are definitely he pieces in my foundation. As result, I definitely feel ready to take the next step in my life and career knowing that I'll be successful.

I have personally found great satisfaction in helping to motivate and empower others. It is natural for a person to go through periods of self-doubt from time to time. Some of the most successful people in the world use "self-talk" to motivate themselves. You might start off thinking it is weird talk to yourself but start off slow and use it when you're working out or doing some physical activity try it and see if it motivates you to do more you will be surprised to see what you can find within yourself. If you are anything like me it will become enjoyable to compete with yourself. Eventually, it will become part of your daily routine and it will give you a better understanding of yourself and your greater purpose in life

# X.

# Reflections

When you read the last chapters of a book people often ask what now? At least that is a question on mind when I read something. People have a natural curiosity for "what's next" and always want to know more. Hopefully by the end of this chapter that question will be answered. I am a person who's "flame" and enthusiasm for life never goes out. I will always have more to give, more to say and I will never stop working to improve myself.

In the beginning of writing this book I had said that one of my goals was to be transparent, genuine and "real". That theme does not end just because this is the last chapter. In the beginning writing this was purely therapeutic, a way for me to express myself. As I got more invested in the process I decided to make this a collection of writings centered on embracing yourself whether you have a disability not. I will be a role model and a voice for people who do not have a confidence to speak up for themselves. You may not believe me but that is a problem that exists in a lot of people not just those of us with "limitations". Everybody no matter who you are has periods of self-doubt where they start to question whether they are doing the right thing in their lives. As I said in the last chapter, "disability" is a man-made concept because struggles don't discriminate I don't care who you are everyone has their challenges. Let this book be a constant reminder to everyone who reads it to embrace life and all its challenges because what we endure make us stronger. A second motivation for writing this book was to show everyone that each person has a gift to share with the world. I am blessed with the ability to relate to a wide range of people and connect with such diverse audiences. I am also fortunate to be able to articulate my words on a page I have always had a passion for writing and connecting with my community on several platforms. This is one of the advantages of having a fire that never burns out . This flame was the catalyst that allowed me to accomplish my goal of becoming an author. I will focus my attention on another worthwhile goal. I want this to be a lesson to everyone that if you set goals you can attain them as long as you never lose your passion for hard work. If you start a project see it through to the end it will come out beautiful. A realization of vision that you can be proud of will be the product of hard work. I wanted this book to be timeless, something that my family, friends in future generations can have as an example of how far the little motivation can take a person if they set goals and don't give up anything is possible. I'm going to use a quote that I brought up in the last chapter because I think it's worth repeating" Don't let people rent space in your head". Put simply if you believe in yourself, that's all that matters. That is a quote from one of my college professors I will never forget. I want this book to be something I can show to my children, a way for them to know how passionate their father was back in his youth.

I have so much to give to the community and to the world this is just one avenue for me to show my passion and motivation. I will take this accomplishment and move forward. I know that there is more for me to do. As I have said several times throughout this book I believe that everybody has a greater purpose and your goal in life should be to find that purpose. Writing this book was a step along the path that will help me find mine, what is yours? Do whatever you can to keep your "fire" burning bright. There will be people who will disagree with you and stand in the way that is just how the world works but, I am confident that you will find a way to overcome it and be a better person as a result of any adversity you may face in your life.

I want this book be a reflection of the feeling I get when I give a presentation to a group. Going back to something I had mentioned in the previous chapter. When you stand in front of an audience and deliver a message as soon as you open your mouth to speak it automatically becomes about the people in the audience it's no longer about yourself. You are sharing yourself and your experience in order to benefit somebody else. It's the most liberating feeling to know that somebody else is smiling because of you. Opening up about your experiences and challenges in life can be hard for some people but when you do it is the ultimate act of selflessness and kindness. You leave hoping that the audience who heard you speak goes home and makes positive change in their life

I'm hoping that this book serves as a reminder to people just how important family and friends are to happiness in life. I personally feel very fortunate that I have been blessed with so many amazing people in my life. The list would be too long if I expressed my gratitude for each one of them. Just know that each one of you is a significant part of who I am. So thank you from the bottom of my heart everyone has helped me become who I am today.

It's very appropriate to start the last section of the final chapter with these words:

"When your legs don't work like they used to before

And I can't sweep you off of your feet

Will your mouth still remember the taste of my love?

Will your eyes still smile from your cheeks?

And, darling, I will be loving you 'til we're 70

And, baby, my heart could still fall as hard at 23

And I'm thinking 'bout how people fall in love in mysterious ways

Maybe just the touch of a hand

Well, me - I fall in love with you every single day

And I just wanna tell you I am

So honey now

Take me into your loving arms

Kiss me under the light of a thousand stars

Place your head on my beating heart

I'm thinking out loud"

-ED SHEERAN

Those lyrics embody essentially what I have been doing throughout the book," Thinking out loud. "Always using my voice, passion and motivation to help others. I feel very fortunate to be in this position to positively impact other lives, I will not stop! I am always thinking of different ways to get ahead and help my community and writing this book is just one of the ways I have found to serve others.

Coming down to the last two and possibly most profound reasons for this book each of the reasons so far have been important but these are the closest to my heart. First off, for anybody who has a sibling whether it is a brother or sister, I want people to cherish the bond that they have with their sibling. I want people to know how much my brother meant to me and to my family. I hope that the people who will never get a chance to meet myself, my brother or my family will get a sense of his compassion and the bond that we shared. Use this as a reminder of how important family is as a foundation to your personal success. Please don't ever forget to thank them for all that they do on a daily basis that contributes to your happiness and your success. It is easy to get caught up in the day-to day monotonous routine and these things can slip our minds but it makes it no less important. We all have to take a step back and appreciate where we are in life because it is truly a gift. If you do not take time to do that how can we ever appreciate what the future holds!  Appreciate the journey because every day is special and life is not a guarantee that's what makes every moment so awesome.

I do not pretend to have all the answers. I do know what works for me. I may talk to myself a lot in order to self-motivate and keep things straight in my own head but if you do these things as a reminder that will help us all to maintain the "big picture of life." I'm not saying it will be easy nothing ever is as we plan it. You will appreciate the journey a whole lot more if you don't sweat the small stuff. I want to leave you with one final thought and close with these lyrics:

Yeah... this right here

Goes out, to everyone, that has lost someone

That they truly loved.


Seems like yesterday we used to rock the show

I laced the track, you locked the flow

Words can't express what you mean to me

Even though you're gone, we still a team

In the future, can't wait to see

If you open up the gates for me.

Reminisce some time


It's kinda hard with you not around

Know you in heaven smilin down


Til the day we meet again

In my heart is where I'll keep you friend

Memories give me the strength I need to proceed

Strength I need to believe

Every time I pray, I'll be missing you


- Sean "Puff Daddy" Combs and Faith Evans

Thank you so much for letting me share my story. It means so much to me, my brother and my family. "Keep It Rollin". Every day forward.... Always forward. I love you Dan... I will see you again I promise.

# Keep It Rollin

# THAT'S THE NAME OF THE JOUNEY